OYO

The Beautiful River

Also by Mark B. Hamilton

100 Miles of Heat [chapbook]

Discovering Home: A Sojourn on the Lewis and Clark Trail by Paddle and Pack Mule [video]

Confronting the Basilisk [poetry collection]

Earth Songs [chapbook]

OYO

The Beautiful River

an environmental narrative in two parts

poems by

Mark B. Hamilton

Shanti Arts Publishing

Brunswick, Maine

OYO The Beautiful River

an environmental narrative in two parts

Published by Shanti Arts Publishing
Interior and cover design by Shanti Arts Designs

Shanti Arts LLC
193 Hillside Road
Brunswick, Maine 04011
shantiarts.com

Cover image: Susan Brownfield, *Sunset.*
Digital representation of an acrylic on canvas.
Used with permission of the artist.

Printed in the United States of America

ISBN: 978-1-951651-37-4 (softcover)

Library of Congress Control Number: 2020942221

dedicated to my sister, Sue,
for her lifelong love of the arts

Contents

Acknowledgements

Many thanks . . .

to the editors of the following publications where these poems first appeared:

Canvas: "An excerpt from 'Fortunate Creek'"

Cider Press Review: "A Levee Town"

The Listening Eye: "A Serious Business," "The *American Dream*, and a Man," "Hands that Row," and "When a River"

Naugatuck River Review: "Raw Moonlight"

New Letters: "The River as Teacher," finalist creative nonfiction

North of Oxford: "Down City," "In City," and "Out City"

Oxford Poetry: "Whistle Creek"

Plainsongs: "Buffalo in the Woods" and "Flotsam & History"

Poetry Salzburg Review: "Horses Crossing the River" and "A Little River Town"

Ship of Fools: "100 Miles of Heat," "An Island in History," "Dreams of Point Pleasant," and "A Fine Sleep"

THINK: "In Contrast"

Third Wednesday: "A Welcoming"

Umbrella Factory Magazine: "Hidden Voices," "Lunch at Harrods," and "Meditation on Light"

The Wayfarer: "Now"

Weber—The Contemporary West: "Chrome & Corners" and "Through Time, the Joyous Ledges"

The Written River: "Of Bayous and Pine Sand"

to Finishing Line Press for the chapbook *100 Miles of Heat*, which first included the poems: "The Estuarial Brain," "Fortunate Creek," "Ohio's First City," and "A Song";

to Walt and Virginia Spurgeon for their friendship and expertise in the building of the rowing dory "Pelican";

to the Mudokwan, and to Grand Master Jong Woo Kim, Muncie, Indiana;

to the Greater Pittsburgh Aquatic Club at Neville Island for the launch of "Pelican" onto the Ohio River; and

to Sandie Seeger for her substantive editing and loving encouragement.

Oh *not* because happiness *exists,*
that too-hasty profit snatched from approaching loss.
Not out of curiosity, not as practice for the heart, which
would exist in the laurel too . . .

But because *truly* being here is so much; because everything here
apparently needs us, this fleeting world, which in some small way
keeps calling to us. Us, the most fleeting of all.

—Rainer Maria Rilke, "The Ninth Elegy"

OYO

SPRING

A Song, Softly Sung

What is strange is often invisible,
and the river was strange.

Unknowns crept up from uncertainty,
flotsam gathered in flood above the dam,
and under the slurry of debris the waves hid
a tragedy with fish scraping their bellies
in the silky silt of its toxic soup.

The world of the fish was a near disaster.
Caught at the end of lines like little nightmares
with jellied flesh, three eyes or deteriorating bones,
their very nature was being altered
beyond the nature of things.

When street lamps had burned all day
like buoys in the smog, and smokestacks
had stood like candles in a gray cloud cake,
a city was called, "Hell with its lid off,"
the horizon drawn in so tightly
it became its own combustion chamber,
a dark purse aflame
with everything melting inside it.

People became lost in the shadows
from the funneling columns of smoke
and stumbled along the ragged edges of a river
where I, too, needed to know where I was
and who I might become,
and yet I knew that my knowing
would be slow, and that any song
I might sing
would be sung softly, if at all.

Now

Time follows like a hound,
like a scent in the wind
in the bushes rushing past.
One is forgotten with the next.
Existence becomes the feeling
of what surrounds.

I become tiny,
the only self-powered craft
on the river, moving near shore,
safely in the shallows
my elbows at the surface.
I'm a part of the river
rather than a power over it.
Where I am is all there was.

Branches swish past in arcs of oars
drawn out from slate green waters,
willows framing red flowers
on the mud glaze, their flared petals
bursting from tangles of shaggy bark
where Neville Island ends in mud shoals
and the sharp pin point of a buoy's
bright light.

Commercial piers stagger out
with names like Standard Laforge
and Buckeye Pipeline Company.
Anxieties keep me poised
upon the immense gray empty.

It is unrushed. And I like it.

With grace and humor
I exit the first lock and dam,

the shoreline etched into clusters
of poles and smokestacks, clanks
of metal and hums from hidden roads.

Under the thud-thud of a pile driver
rust and angularity echo between sheds,
black lines of riverbank becoming wall,
culvert, then ramp and conveyor belt
joining barges to mountains of coal.

The folded silhouette of the dory
lifts over waves like origami
in its simple act along a crease of map,
huge cranes dropping black buckets
as large as dump trucks into the valley
of barge, vibrating, crowding the trees,
rebounding into corrugated warehouses
where rusted roofs slant their pastels
into uninhibited space.

I map the changes from artifact to symbol:
from rickety shack to rusted roofed effigy
swinging its document of tin;
wardrobes falling apart, reconstructed
by the welder's spark;
electrons leaping from their orbits.

I sweep through a landscape
faster and faster, scanning the emptiness
for a meaning, and then for an escape,
wondering if I could stop, or even perceive
of myself as stopped,
etched into the black on white
amid all this clutter.

But questions disappear
at bridges, under the exact grids built
with individual rivets
that divide my crossing in all directions.

Everything ends, and then begins.
Water folds and contorts, pulls down
and boils up, blossoming sideways
until the oars are useless,
the laws of buoyancy suspect
and any sense of place destroyed.

Flotsam & History

Caught in the song
I hurry beneath a hammock of power lines
stretched river-wide at the Crain Brothers dock,
fast currents defined by a storm in upstate
New York and by the squirrels swimming in a furry
bridge remembered from the history books.

A signal light flashes Red, Yellow, then Green,
dropping me down into a concrete box of the lock,
walls speckled with bugs and water fleas—a cascade
aglow with wasps and spider webs.

I am the idle caretaker lulled by soft sounds
sinking into shade with the dory nudging the gray grit
and snugging at the end of its line.

I row out in rhythms through flotsam,
through chucks of wood and Styrofoam
into the mist drifting from the churning froth
of rocks at the foot of the dam,
where trees spin in an apparition of orange,
broken-off, pointed limbs peeled back
like fish held sideways in a snake's mouth.

Then, through the long span of Pennsylvania Power
and the roots tangling out from steep sand banks
where I stop beneath maples hiding bird song
along a river widening into everywhere.

Nothing is wasted. Nothing is denied.
Even the space between heartbeats becomes a pause
where everything just stops, picks-up
and moves on.

WHEN A RIVER

Oar tip to oar tip,
Pelican glides between the pillars
of crafted stone onto a creek
towards a floating dock painted red
on milk chocolate water swirling
with rainbows of dust and road grime.

Misty showers quiet the sky
into sighs of purple and starchy pink.
While across the Ohio, a smokestack
flash burns emissions, its flame leaping up
to waver and burst with ignited gas
sounding like a heavy rug being shaken out.

Near the boat, a beaver stands in the mud
watching me with its intimate eyes,
using little fingernails to munch on a twig.

In the morning I cross over to West Virginia,
to the cabins breathing the air of a pebbly beach,
but my leisurely row becomes a tough pull
as headwinds pile up the river.

Humbled close-in at Cumberland Locks,
Pelican churns and chops, drops from the white caps
marching up the valley.
Under fast wisps of cloud I tack crosswind
angling the blades, feathering each stroke
to corkscrew off the crests.

We buck and shudder in the chilling spray
exhilarated by a rogue wave whooshing beneath
with its warning: "Stay relaxed. Stay in rhythm
with the weather."

A Welcoming

Short Creek swells
into a bay with the new depth of rain—
a fresh, enchanted world all its own.

Within two hundred yards we're amid geese,
sedges, and meadow grasses. The breeze lulls
with its metronome of blackbirds.

And there are water bugs!
and the soft webbings of feet.

So I row upstream, off the map
into rural backyards, then turn to float
through the ponds and grasses again,
carried by reflections—by the musings
of the gods in the marsh.

At midnight, bass begin to rise,
tails and fins bristling like castanets,
flapping against the hull in reckless turns,
plankton, copepods, and water fleas
bursting right up into the stars.

Hidden Voices

The river clears out debris, sifting
and digesting, washing pollutants away.

Recovered in part, the Beautiful River
ushers me along, never losing its dignity,
never complaining nor faltering in its design.

It asks nothing of me, demands no reward,
requires no sacrifice.

Slowly, my adoration grows,
the dory bounding over a steeplechase below
on sounds roiling up from proud waters.

Fish are almost edible, clam and mussel shell
fleck the bank in flickers flying past.

At Boggs Run

In fast water red towboats shuttle empty barges
bank to bank like ants with big black seeds.

Shouldered toward the terminal, I row harder
into shoal waters hugging the opposite bank
like a mouse navigating along the baseboard
of a dance floor. Beneath sweeping arcs of coal
powered wires the red jacketed waiters nod
condescendingly, and a General raises an eyebrow
rattling his sabre above the waltzing shuffle
of big black shoes.

I cross the busy ballroom of a blue-collar river,
the symphony's pit filling with drum and cymbal
crashing against the long piers of Consolidated Coal.

Then I drift away, staying well past,
down to the radical oxbow at the Indian mounds,
and the tall, single smokestack of Edison Electric
coloring-in the sky with its big gray crayon.

Moundsville

The Iroquois called it "Oyo," the Beautiful River,
my intended anchorage an inward channel
rotted and scattered with snags and stumps
slant-cut and rising in shards of deepening dusk.

Bones, beads, and pottery turn in the fields of ash
under a tractor's slow plow moving through the trembling
Earth, easing the loam for the hovering of crows.

Renewed by the sun, I am the farmer, and the merchant
woven from natural threads in a circle of origins
stretched by the six directions.

I tie-off to underwater roots opposite the channel
on a sloped beach of an island, to make my camp
across from hills spilling away into the sunset.

Barn swallows swoop the air
and little brown bats cartwheel their angularities,
the arcs and spirals of the moon and sun
wrestling over the face of the Earth.

Pinks merge with lavenders above sleepy eyelids,
the Adena reclining on their sacred lands, these mounds
of river held in cycles by the apt essence of things.

HANDS THAT ROW

All things on a map are not true:
buoys drift out of place; islands get washed away.

The one sure thing when rowing
is that everything comes down to the hands
etching time into each day
of a changing river.

A beautiful doe, huge ears listening,
nips a few leaves and ambles out of sight,
invisible in that single step beyond the pine boughs.

She knows the river creates through time, not as time,
not as some clock turning into fatigue at day's end.

From her response, my struggle seems too unnatural.
I think I have much work to do.

At Willow Island Dam, the lockmaster says,
"Haven't seen a row boat on this river for twenty-five years!
Where're ya' goin'?"
"Cairo."
"Kayro! Well, that's a ways. Good luck to ya'!"
he says, with a nod and smile.

My body begins to breathe the river, merging
with the countryside, awakening to a rural life of friends
and family staying put, holding the mud down.

A Little River Town

When ashore, nothing is better than a new map,
clean clothes, and fresh fruit beneath a pavilion in the rain.
I prowl the town to favored shops, retaining joy for little things
I need or want: pastry, hamburger, chocolate bar. Showers follow
me around: a picket fence, sidewalk, shade tree, urging me
down a magnolia street.

In the morning, on flat water I row out into the floodplain.
Bass boats skim past, their hulls balanced on their props
ripping growls from the river. The wind dies, the sky darkens
into slate, raindrops approaching in a busy hum.

They close-in like a freight train rattling and boiling,
shrinking the horizon into a mere gap of low cloud, a waterfall
I enter, exhilarated, inside a tin can beneath the heel of thunder.
Flat down, expecting nothing, lightening flashing left
and right, I feel the boldness of the river rumbling,
raindrops popping into craters and leaping fragments.

I lean forward, compressed under the heavy paws, the dory
cutting through vertical water.

And then suddenly, it all stops.
The storm subsides. Its identity of an hour the refreshing
cool water swashing around my ankles—the cycle of weather
melding with greens and silvers in the loom of trees.

A red-headed buzzard, brooding in the branches,
hunches its shoulders, the air so clear each feather
seems edged by a single thread.

OHIO'S FIRST CITY

Marietta sits on knolls above the Muskingum
where I nestle into a transit slip at the City Marina,
my hands wrapped and blistered, especially the left
which is vengeful.

Towboats pass—those prone statues sleeping
on their backs—a melted quarter mile of scrap iron
or an island of heaped coal.

I am a river roustabout in a rag cap and baggy breaches
strolling the corridor of cars and glass shops, pleased
with the company I keep in this vast amusement park.

A fisherwoman casts her lure into the mysteries, into shadows
of a moored sternwheeler, the showboat *Becky Thatcher.*

She weaves a question and retrieves the chance,
breathing above the sighs of the Muskingum.

Marietta watches, close to sleep,
resting on the ancient geometry of the Adena.

An Island in History

The channel line sways from riverbank
to riverbank as I maneuver in the wakes of towboats
looking always to escape, to jump out of the dory
onto shore immersed as I am in this commerce of Lime,
Metal, Oil, and Aggregates.

I practice aggression, the boldness of a red-tailed hawk
diving out of the heated sky into a clutch of ducks
scooting around in the shallows.

The current drags me through the narrows at Neal Island.
In two hours ten miles pass amid kingfishers and towboats
thumping toward Parkersburg Bend and the Little Kanawha River.

For Lewis, squirrels kept migrating across the Ohio,
and sunsets were dimmed by great flocks of passenger pigeons.
His crewmen, arriving late that morning, were rounded up bodily,
too drunk to depart. Malaria was endemic,
the U.S. Postal Service just a man billeted in a clapboard house
where Lewis joined him for dinner behind window panes
in the candlelight.

At Blennerhassetts Island, the once fine gardens are scattered
with black walnut trees, the mansion burned down by slaves.
Harman and Margaret were Aaron Burr supporters, plotting
for new territories in the west with that sly General Wilkinson.
And it is said, she still gallops her horse along the river at night,
wearing a red ballroom gown that flows like fire.

I walk westward, behind my heart through hayfields,
up into the meadows of sunshine thinking of them
and of history in the dust of a dirt road to a log cabin
where kids are playing with a pet raccoon.

Beneath cool cottonwoods, I sit and eat, and then launch from the beach to head downriver again, well off the channel with my feet up as I drift and snooze in the heat, sheltered by the wide brim of a straw hat.

A Song

Today I've left the city,
its jowly air and its brittle air
in the murk of shouldering streets.

I've cast away most of the weight
carried in my pockets. Like the tarp
I slide beneath, I'm freed.

The Ohio wind is a soothing wind,
and I row to my heart's content,
a maple clutching the muddy bank
holding messages I've sent.

Today, I've left the city
and row to my heart's content.
for I think I need to know that voice
of what the river meant.

Horses Crossing the River

Hazardous herds of wild mustangs
chiseled in the stream loom up from the shallows,
pointed ears like saw teeth, the horses crossing
in textures unaccustomed to these soft greens.

Near Shade River, I land at a smooth beach
beyond a rocky point. With the first step I'm in deep mud,
quicksand up to my thighs, a hand on Pelican lifting me free.
Under the heat, the "to and from" seem all the same.

An island towhead, packed hard with sand, has drift
in crotches of trees thirty feet up and stuffed with debris
in a sensible ruin from all the spring flooding.

At Sandy Creek the browns and greens flicker golden
opaque light, my small boat solid and low in the water,
nestled so closely that dark maples turn blue to indigo.

Through Pelican's hull I hear a gurgling,
then hushed voices—three teenagers drift-fishing,
their outboard engine barely audible at idle.

It is nightfall on the slow flow. Muskrats are out. They belly
down the bank, cruise by and browse on tender vegetable things,
thinking me a pretty fancy log surrounded by water bugs
and not too many mosquitoes.

I think I could live here, close to the river, in a cabin
on stilts all year long.

It's amazing how far we will travel
to understand just one old saying.

Dreams of Point Pleasant

I row with the left hand tingling,
the palm no longer useful, only the last knuckles
of each digit functioning. By day's end
my extremities are numb.

Yet the world goes well here,
although a nice breeze would be welcomed
as more than a thought in the trees,
or the dust above a hay field, or the silence
of a heron stalking its own image.

In the drowse of afternoon
I drift past four teenage girls splashing
in the shallows, water nymphs releasing me
from my efforts, just another bird of reflection.

On open water, in heavy rain
I row beneath my red hat to a bridge
that crosses a creek where rusty run-off
forms a waterfall, a haven where I anchor,
close-in to the riprap, and snug between
the sunken re-iron and a grappling hook.

Flooding would change the safe nature of this place.

In the morning, my oar strokes are in higher water,
reflections rushing forward in a rhythm of color
enlivened by the rippling wake.

Deep in the curve of creek, the wooded banks
on either side, I'm close to the hush of bird song,
a quietude that turns into a mystery, the ancient myths
submerged like fallen trees.

I pass a West Virginia power plant, the turbines
humming ominous and linear, the implacable jaws
of a crane's bucket dropping into a barge and lifting
the transformations of the sun.

Near Point Pleasant, I row into a labyrinth of creek,
of tangled ponds and clinging branches, the painted turtles
etched along its sides like a map, a ramp cluttered with drift
and litter, the old dock inundated, tilted and waterlogged
with its weight of liverworts.

I row until I begin to feel lost, then turn back,
finding the new ramp and its dusty parking lot
where two boys are fishing amid plastic soda bottles.

My dreams of clean clothes, a shower, and a few days
off the river, end at a nearby convenience store with its
treasure chest of ice cream bars.

And I struggle not to be disappointed with this confluence
where the Ohio meets the Big Kanawha River
draining a major watershed of West Virginia,
where I notice how things swept down from the past
of one become the future of the other.

In Contrast

I think I'll just rest.
I think I'll stay at anchor and watch the kids
swimming after ducks. On Sunday, I'll ease out
from the Boat Club, my hands still wrapped but healthy.

I'll drift into the thump-thump of towboats
on the tan wide river, and float through a green countryside
under a soft pattering of rain.

The gentle June flood will usher me along, beyond the map,
but I'll still be here, just too small to be a symbol
charted on the unknown landscape.

It will be me, in a boat, in the spring, on the water
near the shore beneath the warming of a big blue sky.

Beyond the gunnels, trees will walk on the crest of hills,
whistling, their hands in their pockets, my mind scattered
in the meadow like a flock of feeding birds.

Things that used to be will be, and the fat catfish will stir
in the silt of denuded banks, while rain clouds thunder
across into the stillness of West Virginia.

The river will heighten and widen, becoming shaggy
like an animal with teeth and claws that leaps against its chain.
A rusty barge will break free from its mooring.

Tall trees will fly past, undermined by the storm upstream,
gnarled roots hoisted like flags, their half-submerged trunks
speeding away faster and faster.

On the rising current, I'll row hard to a marina
and land on its twisting dock, my nerves a-jangle for hours,
watching the blue-collar river surging past
power plants near sleepy river towns.

Factories will seem warm, even friendly;
flare stacks will be graceful under their billows of vapor,
those thin blankets covering the land;
while children half-asleep will hear their parents
going off to work in little clouds of muffler smoke.

It will be the storm, and the coming of the storm.

A Serious Business

Eating is a serious business, yet hunger forgives a lot.
Repetition and simplicity is the key.
Potable water the premium,
so bring extra for those long stretches and never
use creek or river for kitchen or bath.

And remember, the heft and momentum
of a well-provisioned boat comforts like the body
designed for weather.

I set and sweep, gliding on the flat black creek.
Then, with a joyful ringing, I fairly gallop downriver
past willows and saplings combed by wet colors
of bark and leaf, by soft shelled mud turtles, slick
and vicious, clamoring off tangles of Kentucky debris.

Approaching a ninety-degree turn, I cross to the right,
but the river begins to have a difficult time bending
around the bend. It piles up, folds back, gets in its own way,
the turbulence hiding a sandbar surprisingly submerged
on the outside of the turn.

Waves start to tumble beneath the surface, energies bunch up
for a mile, shearing off into tall crests of escalator waves
undercut from below. I surge and surf down their slopes,
the bow rising from the troughs into ridges of blue sky,
until the river broadens, becoming calm and hot again.

The shoreline whispers, "Sleep. Sleep," but I don't.

CASTLES & DRAGONS

Druids have built turrets for the castled city
to keep the dragon at bay. When the siege ends
gates lift with tongue-and-groove, so people
can return to the river through tiny breaks in a levee,
so small and far I need directions.

At night, we sit around a fire pit
exchanging river news like kids telling ghost stories:
tales of accident, speed, human error, no time to judge,
inexperience, or just plain bad luck that creeps up
into a tragedy.

People keep saying, "You've got to be careful.
You can't believe that you know for sure
because that's when the river will get you."

A full moon reflects the valley,
a towboat moves on distant water, and a couple strolls
the river bank, while others stay to drink
more cold beer in the humid air.

The sun casts no shadows of its own.
The river falls, and is expected to fall even more,
so I leave early, immersed all day by forested hills,
close-in on the strong current.

Skiffs with canopies drag long-line treble hooks
for mussels. Each one chunked into a wire basket:
the precious pigtoe, heelsplitter, or pocketbook.

And the river sprawls, lounging on its back
seemingly asleep, but quick to awaken in the shrubbery
that flutters through its claws.

Like a duckling on fast water, I'm as still as prey
startled by the ballistic surfacing of a channel buoy
popping-up like a cork, then being dragged under
by a tree caught sideways in its mooring chain.

They appear and disappear in a wild gasping.

THE QUIET ART

Like a cool breeze
over a passionate belly,
I lean and bend
frisking over the swells.

Pelican flies past pointed roofs,
red shingles rippling into song,
plants parading in light steps
along ledges of shiny rock.

Obion, a Coast Guard tender,
rushes upstream, called to battle
the wilding tree
wound around the channel buoy's
anchor chain.

Bent spikes gnaw
like teeth in the hungry river;
bobwhites call from the shade
of another straw hat day.

I drift on the quiet
of just being here,
and gaze back occasionally
at something red, something
curiously wrong that floats so high
and moves so quickly.

I wait
in a series of guesses,
until it becomes
an igloo icebox broken
on a river that must be half crow.

A Fine Sleep

Rowing an island hillside
to a rope swing

I rest with heat lightening.
Pelican tugs at the line.

The surge of night
so deepening and wide

A silver carp spins
beneath the moon onto its side,

The river inhaling the light
as it leaps across the sky.

Earth covers in silence
the darkness of dreaming.

Up City

In the heat trees pass slowly.
There are no bird songs, just a few drops of rain.

In the town of Ripley, Civil War cannon
sit on shelves of knick-knack shops, and a museum
for tobacco smells just like my grandfather's barn.

Slipping out beneath slats of sunrise, I row all day,
night descending like gauze into darkness and worry
until I see a dock in the fog, a man and boy fishing
quietly in the quiet.

Next morning they say, "Stay safe!"

By afternoon I stop to walk and stretch my legs
on a newly oiled two-lane road, heat rising from the tar,
orange and blue flowers sparkling in the pasture grass.
Along a barbed wire fence that glints from post to tree
I lean softly into the turns, hovering above the asphalt.

A red flick catches my eye, a large snake
flashing its tongue, probing some deeper tar,
its mouth sensing me, the curve of its thick tail and body
disappearing into the weed stems.

I stand in a din of insects spinning above the meadow.
I listen to the fenced-in wild flowers beneath a hot blue sky.

Downriver, the up-city of Cincinnati collides into wakes,
builds up and topples over with powerboats on washboard
poundings as I jab at the jagged yellow waves adjusting
each stroke to changing depths—a gyroscope in synch
with the circling of southern heat.

In City

As soothing as a tomb
lingering from the night, commuter cars vibrate
the massive brownstone piers of Covington Bridge.

I skim the shadows
near floating cafés where an occasional cook gazes out,
elbows on the railing, flipping a cigarette
with the slightest of nods as we pass.

Sunlight thrums,
begins to hum along the rusted railroad trestle
high above imagined dinners glittering with expense
only the few could afford.

Cincinnati starts to vanish
into rough corrugations zoned commercial downstream,
the earth heaping into scattered clumps and mounds,
into sand and aggregates scattered with tanks of petroleum
from Ashland and Chevron, and a conveyor belt
feeding dust into a cloud above a single, pickup truck.

Down City

Silt and grit
simmer in pools speckled with flecks
of metal and globs of oil.

Water churns in a commerce of sunlight
channeling earth organs, filtering wastes
through kidneys of spongy mud.

The city slows into sediments, into layers
of liquid dumps devoid
of what I need or want, as I row and row
to win it back.

I make a seat.
I set a table below the swing of my arms,
my hands touching her hands.

Trees become glimpses, then whispers.

Out City

A distant cluster of factories hidden in the haze,
the white-walled asphalt plants camouflaged in vapor.

I'm surrounded by rainbows of oil
swirling at the confluence of the Great Miami River
yawning with its brown and dirty yellow tongue,
exhaling fumes from a city's sewage overflow, on storm
waters spewing purulent songs even insects cannot hum.

Webbed branches of a cavern arc and bend, limp
and drooping roots in a soggy murk sprung and wrung
above the lengthening stretch of mud stench.

Unnamed things scatter across the surface,
away from a floating bloated carcass of a cow that rocks,
swaying with blotches and humps in the refuse.

And except for a mosquito
revving its wings past my ear, I hesitate to even touch
the oars to it.

WHISTLE CREEK

Melted by the weight of coal, barges sink low in the water.
Others leave a raft of debris as they pivot from shore.

I pole through floes of clinging wood
into a wreckage of sunset, onto reflected open petals
blossoming from a creek.

Carp nibble the green line of algae along the boat.

But there is no rush; no extra chores to dry things out.
All becomes peaceful and quiet. Here, where everything
is worth having.

Today, my hands became her hands.

SUMMER

BUFFALO IN THE WOODS

I hitch a ride in a rattling-apart jeep
and bounce along the buffalo trace
in rusted jumblings of metal plates.

Protected remnants of an ancient sea
are the sinks of Big Bone Lick
where Captain Lewis collected tusks,
and femurs of mammoth and sloth,
his crewmen boiling brine to scale the salt
from three-legged iron cauldrons.

I pick blackberries on a wooded path
spooking a large red buck into whistling
as he vaults from his afternoon nap
crashing through the underbrush
with a hint of the great migrations.

In generations of horn and hoof
small herds of buffalo are shaggy hills
moving shadows in the forest shade,
the ground rising up around them,
their bright eyes like brown marbles
in a world once balanced by change.

RIVER IN THE BLOOD

I row into the distance, stretching memories
into those finer threads of remembrance.
In the glowing warmth of morning
the elegance of a widening river elapses into hours.

But time is not always an easy measure.
Each day I wander down its moving surface. Each night
I dream with it slipping away. Days merge with days.

Once I had accustomed myself to the work
my hands strengthened to the task, my senses alive
to the bone. Simplicity was in the going,
my spirit in the breeze.

I watched the silt-fluted anchor rise from its little cove.
I waited for the iron gates of Markland Locks to open.

Echoes came out of the rusted treasure chest,
moans from the opening jaws of the whale.

The Death of Clowns

There is no humor in a buck's head, bobbing
expressionless in the backwater, the torn throat
of a towboat throttle growling, nudging the bank,
nor in the afternoon heat where a macabre cartoon
of cowled monks waits in the bleachers, fluffing
in the branches—the vultures crowded into a tree
or hunched over floating fuel signs that point
to hidden gas docks somewhere up the creek.

There is no mirth, or mercy in the glaze of afternoons,
the reflections bending at their waists in cummerbunds,
baldheads, and red fleshy hoods flopping to one side
as they spread their boney pirate wings. For those
are true weapons to tear the soft bellies of the dead.

I row away to avoid the smell,
but there is death to the left, and death to the right,
and more straight ahead on the flat wide river—dozens
and dozens of evenly spaced fish floating belly-up
in little whirlwinds of stench. For half a mile the air
is filled with decay, so at first I think net fishermen
must have created this banquet, but then realize it is
the fish kill from the city's overflowing sewage
diluting slowly down from the Great Miami River.

From the shade, they glide on wings from high limbs
to prod and tug at the flesh, bracing their entire bodies
into huge backward lunges of feathery tuggings,
while others, tired by the competitive eating, are resting
on perches as happily as spectators in the bleachers
of a traveling circus—the spinning, leaping harlequins
in baggy pants heaped into piles, like dead clowns.

SUN, TREES, COAL AND WIRE

At sunrise with a flick of the wrist to feather the blades,
I arc my back to set the oars in silver water close to shore.

Sirius clouds and roosters at dawn frolic in the tangled finery.
A woodchuck, sprawling belly down, dangles its paw and leg.

I stay well clear of iron grates suckling the cooler river raw
and pass beneath tight power lines slung high in a wired sky.

The thirsty turbines drink the water churning into steam, spin
with light from ancient elements old coal into our realities.

My neck stiffens, my arms drawn taut. I pass a clump of mossy
rock beneath cicada wings, the burnt leaves rattling in the wind.

I flee the heat with oars of spruce quivering like the paddlefish
that leap, or drop out of synch, like tilted ceremonial stones.

River of the Heart

I stop for lunch with shells on a beach:
the orange tooth and polished helix of snail;
the saw edged ridge on a black-lined clam.
Then, I push out onto the flat river, again.

Behind an island, I'm chorded-in, nestled
into a logjam. A ski boat skirts with long slalom runs
to test the strength of its weave.

Chiseled into pieces, the wind skips over the wake,
a cat's paw slicing slim bits from the fleshy rolling.

Near the dory, sunfish are tail-flipping,
flinging water up into the boat, into my eyes,
and onto the map.

They are the bubbling cauldron,
or the earth valves of my leaky heart.

MEDITATION ON LIGHT

A curious yellow warbler
tilts its head, skips and flits closer
inspecting my breakfast.

I must be its prime duty of the day,
this bit of tufted sunlight
guiding me through its secret place.

The sunrise inhales intricate leaves,
moist curves of misty shadow.
All this created, not only for me,

But as a part of me.
Pelican glides on amber light,
oar tips dripping, the hull rippling.

The bronze surface, a river town
with windows above little gardens,
and the shearing wake of a towboat

Intent on landing at the new pier
of the Crushed Stone Company.
In shoal waters of the suburbs

I surf the crest and ride the power,
then slog through heavy headwinds
to placid waters of Harrods Creek.

Lunch at Harrods

A waiter stands with a tray of clinking drinks.
Lightening cracks and shakes with thunder.
People stop eating. All are hushed above their plates.

Only one boat is on the river, a white sail, a sloop
reaching across and away. It must be the *Morgan Truce*.

A dark storm strikes center stage,
tragic skies break purple to gray, the rain releasing
far to the east. Not a drop more on Harrods Creek.

Not a breath more on the wide Ohio.

THE FALLS

Vanishing, the river drops forty feet
into a box canyon of cement
squeezing my hands into fists.

I crawl along a small sand island
tying-up to its sweeper pine
to rest, the dory swishing back
and forth like a fishing lure.

I try again, and ascend the pine,
then turn to cross on thick green water
toward the middle where a great rock
cradles me in its eddy.

By nightfall, I'm anchored, safely
in a creek that squiggles on the map
with its secret rookery of herons.

An Unnamed Creek

Rolling over and over inside my cocoon,
I doze beneath dry maples in a deep muddy "V"
opening to the steep slick curves of rusty silt
on either side from where I plan to embark
into a wildlife refuge beneath the Falls.

I exit the creek, revving the dory's buoyancy,
moving up a staircase of pines reflected on smooth
Teflon water that skims down from a dyke line,
my spirits rising on its flat wedge.

Grasping huge chunks of luscious green water
the dory becomes an arrow, the oars my spruce bow.
Each nerve and fiber loosed upon the stairway,
each motion a wisp of white silk on fast black water.

The dory nudges above the surge of the landing.
The boat stays low, the oars held high, my life
vest flashing orange as we're spewed back down
the chute like a watermelon seed.

The stern catches the eddy of the middling rock.
Water boils around me like a flock of wild ducks
swirling into simple laughter.

A Floodplain

I hike across the muddy earth
to shiny rocks polished by glaciers,
to a sea bed littered with flowering
fossils of the chitin's rippling shadow.

How Lewis must have questioned
this crystalline junkyard.
How Clark must have conjured
from these armored stones.

The Refuge nuzzles up
to the Falls into a froth, diluted
by the Upper Ohio crashing down,
where waterfowl still migrate
to nest amid the jagged fossil rock,
and the rare songbirds
still cling to the crevasses
with the daredevil plants.

Here, where the promise lingers
hoping to be remembered.

LOOKING CLOSER

Frogs are silent canaries
in the coal mines of the Ohio

While Shiva glides above the Falls,
a goddess of recycling.

Fish can be eaten, but only in ounces
weighed for their content of PCBs.

And rats get bred as test animals,
although mink are the more sensitive.

So I wonder, should these tests
be more pet or pest

While Shiva glides above the Falls?

I slice through a curtain of nettles.
A man warns me off with his rifle.

Thieves are stealing outboard engines,
and I'm a stranger at his road's end.

Skirting the sinks, I balance atop logs.
A country gent, propped up on an elbow,

Stretched out in an insolence of repose—

A channel buoy on the hill's leafy mold
flaunting its broken chain.

THROUGH TIME, THE JOYOUS LEDGES

Where moss and grass brush velvet over moist slate,
where patches of ferns flare and each breath descends
to the water, and below into the jabbering grottos,
the frescos painted by plants in broad strokes,

Cliffs sing of the diminishing shade, and of flecked edges
slowing quick water into a long descent that strengthens
into the distance, smoothed by the journey of its new voice.

Copper-gold pours into the basin, a shallow bowl held
by bristles etched within the fringe of sharp branches,
and there is no stopping it, this widening of no shade
along the arm of a flat river.

So sometimes, I envy speedboats shrinking that distance,
their windshields in the breeze, hair flying, sweat cooling,
the hull speeding into space with just a flick of its wheel,

Because rowing is different. At three mph I feel the shifting
water lean from place to place, the earth tilting and altering
the river's speed and course.

My eyes see details in dusty leaves, in bottle caps and bugs,
my nose tests the air, my ears the deep hum of factories,
the bird call, or the jet ski high-cycling over its own wake,
each oar stroke searching the murk, sensing those wild
adaptations in an energy of flow.

"Use was never the first truth," says Momaday.

A caramel doe arches her neck and watches
from behind a tender pine. Then another, browsing, nibbles
on a low shrub. More heads lift from the hidden creek,
then, an entire herd moves beyond the rise, all their smooth
fur concealed by that single step into the afterglow.

OTTER CREEK

All wealth hides beyond the stone piers of an old trestle
spanning the zigzag of creek, alluding to industrial ruins.

The eddy, at the foot, captures a carcass—a fresh skinned
beaver, the spine knuckled white under its burnt orange flesh.

Gliding through a tunnel of trees, I breathe the flood that tugs
the shore scattered with milky webs and 'No Hunting' signs.

Otter Creek narrows, twists and turns into a valley sloping up
from cottonwoods dangling their soft roots into the stream.

It is a hungry place—a stomach, and a sanctuary of appetite,
a playground of need for eating, excreting, and breeding.

Voices of frog and cries of other small animals fill the air;
hooves break branches, and wetlands move up into the sky.

Refreshed in glimmers and reflections, a fallen docile tree
bridges the separate worlds, carries light from there to here.

Beavers ghost-by, their pointed ears above glassy round eyes:
water-hog heads lifted; whiskers streaming; toes wide spread.

I feel accepted, or perhaps ignored, until I drop the saucepan lid
and the fat tails slap down like big flat rocks dropped from trees

Disconnecting everything: turtle from branch, insect from twig,
all the unseen disappearing in a valley that awakens like a womb.

That morning, the newspaper is "Geese!"—a fluffy gaggle
that hurries alongside, paddling under my wet wooden wings.

THE AMERICAN DREAM, AND A MAN

Sometimes, life is more than we expect.

The paddlewheel, *American Dream,*
was hard aground on a bar near Troy, yet now
entertains guests and journalists with champagne.

Embattled, she proceeds. People line the shore
to encourage and celebrate. Her dance card is full.

So when she's due at the town's little quay,
I give Pelican a good scrub down, and we wait.

But the lady is late, so I sit in the dory watching
shapes change from sharp to smooth, gravel to sand,
and listen to the high limbs scraping across the sky.

I glimpse a rock, or a strange stump that widens
into conflicting angles and colors unusual to see,
the arcs of rusty orange, or the unfamiliar charcoal.

Edging closer I start to imagine, or think that this
might be a body in the water, in the shade, a bit bulging
into an arc of back, the hump of a male possibly
in the smudge of spine, the head shaven to pinpoints
or buzz-cut to a butch.

I cannot make sense of it. But the rising of the forearms
at the elbows, the hands curling inward toward the head,
the floating buttocks, and the round bulge of the calf.

Probably a manikin, some tom-foolery of a river scamp.

It's too incredible to be real. But the legs, the bulbous heel,
the creases of skin at the arch, my eyes widening into a body
with arms outstretched, feet tapping sadly on the driftwood.

I should report it. I can't abandon it.
I should attach a float, so it won't get lost.
I should call the Coast Guard. But no one answers.
No one comes. No one is listening for my emergency call.

Finally, the State Police arrive,
and the County Coroner confirms it is not a hoax.

He had wandered away from his nursing home.
He had done it before. His son had become anxious and notified
city police. And yesterday, his clothes were found neatly folded
on the river bank in some fragile heaven of concern.

I row into the afternoon, far into the curve of rolling hills
into an amphitheater of hewn benches forming the stone valley,
cliffs of barren pinks and greens merging fast with dusk.

Like a cloud, the *American Dream* glides by,
ornate stacks flaring black crowns, the decks white porticoes
and verandas with aperitifs tilted in the crescent wings of angels,
the paddlewheel churning a wake into spume.

My intended anchorage is an island awash with currents
sweeping through saplings and combing over gravel,
so I row back to Blue River where the sky opens to the east,
just me, the *American Dream*, and a man.

Fortunate Creek

The dragon leans through the oxbow,
curves through the steep valley of rock, past variations
of table, bench and shelf, beneath the hammock of crest line,
along the sloped sky etched into a dorsal ridgeback.

Hills play high in the meadows with oak and pine,
shadows jumping from rock to sky, tracing their silhouettes
into verticals and plateaus to an isolated house with children
laughing on its big red porch.

I move below on reflections in an early morning breeze
where gray goats flit over gray rocks, chased by a shepherd
in a skiff whose engine smokes along the trotline, fish buoys
checked, hauled-in, and baited, the valley widening
into a sandy floodplain for picnics, tents, and ski boats.

It feels good to sweat and row the miles in a frisky wherry
through hay country and cornfields absorbing the heat,
weaving the switchbacks, breathing the river.

Creeks do not tempt my imaginings. Sand appears
and disappears into brush and bush as I row past terminals
abandoned by the river, the river calling me on and on.

By dusk, it seems I'll need to anchor out with the towboats.
I've been caught by late evening without a safe place to stop:
undercut banks are ten feet high, small creeks mere sloughs,
so I cross the river towards Yellow Bank Creek, farther on.

Dusty foliage and swishing twigs sweep water into a swath
where I suspect the entranceway to the creek lies, under the hem
of green tapestry.

I pull at the leaves' sharp edges. I drag through, breaking limbs
without a choice, expecting a dreary anchorage dingy with bugs
and snakes, until I fall out into the light, into a tremendously

gracious pond surrounded by duckweed, where the sky
stretches the long white anchor line taut.

Minnows rattle across the shallows—a miniature squall line
rippling over the surface with sunfish in hot pursuit,
and a gar poking its snout out, snorkeling the length of a log.

Towboats thump and clank upriver, passing the sunset,
pressure waves surging into the pond beneath the dory
and scattering Sirius clouds into thin flakes as orange as coals,
the night lingering into purple and disappearing into ink.

If I could name this place, I would name it Fortunate Creek,
for it has calmed my anxious heart.

The Estuarial Brain

I wake to a rooster, and to insects pelting the canvas,
a blizzard of mayflies tic-ticking, massing above and around,
nicking one another with their wings, the air filled
with percussions of flight from shore to shore.

Up and back, along the creek and into the maples,
the water is covered with their casings.

Last night the larvae, the *subimagos* emerged.
This morning the males are swarming, the females darting-in
to be mated by the chemistry in a clasping of desire.

After a year, the burrowing nymphs have tired of eating algae
deep in silt, and they've burst out into flight, having molted
during the night to replenish the spirit of this place.

Mayflies in amber gossamer—the strength of 300 million years
lifting from the creek, guided by the moon and sun in swaths
clattering their emergence, their Eros of silt from mud love.

Netted wings swarm each to each binding in beauty the tender
fossil beats, their insect intellects conjoining one to one, each
node a click of tiny fluttering, a synapse of an estuarial brain.

I watch until the final few rattle up into leaves of dry maple,
heat rising above farmland to usher me farther downstream,
my straw hat regaining its yesterday's shape.

At Millstone Creek, people are moving in dusk and dream,
children running and shouting amid mushrooms of bright tents
with sparklers and roaring roman candles as they celebrate
the Fourth of July with zinging rocket poppers over open water,
with dissolving flares and pinwheels and campfires.

I anchor along a secluded bank, the frogs a chorus of mud
rib-bitting up and down the inky dark, singing their madrigal:
Rib-Bit, Rib-Bit. Rib-Bit, Rib-Bit.

Every five or six feet a new voice rising up
into a green dot on the imagined shore.

Rib-Bit, Rib-Bit. Rib-Bit. Crunch-Crunch.
A raccoon chimes in with its musical pause.
The universe keeps spinning, frogs going 'round and 'round.

CHROME & CORNERS

Leisurely campers rouse to feed their fires,
dry maples flashing up in the narrow sky, the oars bent
white on the bright mirror of creek as I exit.

A hidden wind begins to buffet the dory.
Forced toward the rocks, waves crowd the boat like puppies,
one jumping in with its bucket of water, wagging its tail
and curling around my feet.

Golden boulders on the weathered shore
gather into shadow, where moist coils of monofilament
tangle in chunks and shreds of cut bait. I crab cross-wind,
to edge away, struggling to gain the lee and clear the point.

On shaky legs I land at an old marina,
walking up to the motel with the storm coming.
It's a quick smudge of black sky on the southern horizon.

From inside, it looks tame—just lightening, thunder
and strong sheets of rain.

Pelican tugs at the lines. The air mixes with sulfur
from a paper mill over in Kentucky.

"It smells like this with the storms," the manager says,
worried about the lateness of this year's fishing season.
"I'm usually filled up by now, but it's late, late, late,"
she says, handing me the key and showing me around.

Alone with bunk beds and walls, I cook and eat.
Then walk along the river in gusts of rain, and do laundry
in a white room full of chrome and corners.

THE OHIO CHANGES

Water speeds up in a canyon, slows down in a gorge,
then meanders (as it should) through a widening oxbow
of colors with shadows sweeping past granite boulders
shattered into rough outcroppings of mica.

I skirt ridges and shorelines, entering the floodplain
enthused by the distance, by the large farms and houses,
hay fields and cities, and the occasional far voice diminishing
at the skyline, the river unfolding like a fan.

And it keeps altering, this widening, into other new sounds
like a drum head thrumming echoes to its sprawling change,
to a pulsing acoustic of habitat in the expanding topography.

Lowlands lift hot winds into a sky that fractures blue
reflections into shards, bursting the mirror from its sluice.
And there are wings of crows in diesel fumes that fade
into shimmering whispers of ancient oceans in the heart.

At Indiana-Michigan, twin turbines eat mountains of coal,
sumping river water down thermal throats until the concrete hums,
smokestacks exhaling the quivered air into a mirage of mantis
mandibles tearing flesh—the crane operator hunched in prayer.

Inside the fly bulb eyes, levered fingers squish the juices
around colossal legs as industry moves in to the town of Rockport
where I climb a wooden staircase cabled and bolted to a cliff face,
above to a vista—where the Ohio is singing a forever song.

Of Bayous and Pine Sand

How like a river can a river be
When a river even changes in thought?

Listen to it whisperin', whisperin'
Listen to it whisperin' wide.
Listen to the river rattlin'
When the towboats go rattlin' by.

The river from my top most window
Wakens to the changin' season, too.
The winter-wild river white and icy
Beneath the stone slow blue.

How like a river can a river be
When the river even changes me?

I pass the first swamp. Coal, utilities, and aggregate companies
dot the shore, and a terminal juts out solely for molasses.

"Hey, Jakes! Yah. How ya' doin?! Good, good. Yah, this is Annie
up at Neville Island. Yah. Say, hey Jakes, listen. Could you send
a 3 x 5 tow of molasses? Yah. The folks here in Pittsburgh
want to make some gingerbread. Yah, that's right. Throwing
a big shindig. In about a week? OK. Wonderful. No. No,
we'll get that from Wisconsin, across and down the Allegheny.
They're already stampedin' the cows. Right. You too, Jakes!"

Southern heat greets me at Owensboro
in the guise of a wooden dock dried to a pulp,
so evaporated that even the red paint stands up on end.
All the nails drawn out by the claw hammer of the sun.
Only an artist's rendering holds it in place.
Tetanus shots are given free with dockage.

And it also has no shower, and no restroom.
Not because of the heat, or perhaps because of the heat.

But I'm glad to be here anyhow, safe and secure,
tied to a marina where I can sleep tonight
with the catfish fishermen fishing, drifting past
on the multicolored city lights.

Slowly, I adapt. Change works through my anxieties,
layers my personality, laminates my body like a truss.
New knowledge creeps over the bridge with its tonnage,
heat absorbs into my skin, sinking down to my melted bones.

I skirt the left bank of a pebble-studded earth
listening for a rhythm of river, noting the music between
dry leaves. There is hardly any current when a plowing tow
catches me with its wake along a string of fleeted barges.

I angle toward a gap, a missing tooth in the outer line,
dragging the oars to brake the ride, surging through, but cornered.
I pull hard, turning on a dime just short of old barge # 397,
after the expert cue shot by the passing towboat captain.

"He sure was in a hurry. Probably, delivering that molasses."

I boll weevil out 'a there, away from all those rusty dents,
and take a salt pill, drink some water. I've lost lots of weight,
and it's difficult to row for an entire day. My mind creeps away.
By 9 A.M., I'm into the heat of afternoon.

So I've learned to plan each day as a ritual focused on the going,
and occasionally I'm rewarded with what I call, "an emergence"
from the depths, a thought or experience that seeks its image
at the surface—becoming my serenity in a breezy kind of joy.

I land at French Island Marina to lunch under a tree
that I've studied for hours as an approaching spot of shade,
but Pelican nips at the tether and leaps along the dock.
From a distance the marina was calm and cool, framed
and hung on a wall of sky where I've skipped out of time.

Memories begin to merge and dissolve.

Even towns, locks and dams disappear, stretching
back into the vague horizon, weaving bits of frayed tapestry
from morning to noon to night.

So I celebrate each threshold with treats and float breaks, selecting
the best anchorage I can predict. One day becoming the next.

Engaged with this southern river, I try not to battle it
in spite of all my protective imaginings,
here, where there are no sights or sounds of birds any more
in Audubon country, just the immense concrete walls
of Alcoa and Southern Gas & Electric
rising into a near cathedral under a continual heft of heat.

BEST BEACH ON THE OHIO

The hull's white paint stained
tan to the gunnels gets scrubbed
with brush and handfuls of sand.
Pelican tips and careens as I rub
its transom, false keel, and stub snout,
no longer a wooden wok for carp
nibbling green meals at the waterline.

I take long breaks with wading birds
and eat a big orange under the sun.

O for this gritty life!
a world clean and healthful.
How I wish it were true.
How I'd walk out into the vision,
into the waves rushing onto the beach,
my toes digging down into a coolness
of clam.

Without a choice, I'd eat the fish.
Without a choice, I'd drink the water.
I'd even breathe the water
where the least terns dive, spiraling
into splashes of little white flowers,
the sun-dazzled waves lapping
onto a hearth of beach like hope.

But, I am as ambivalent
as a sawyer sawing
wondering how I got so far
down the river all of a sudden.

RAW MOONLIGHT

Light teases the brittle fringe of shadow
that lies upon the creek stretching each sliver of moon
that blinks from its moist yoke,
frogs croaking amid late night camp voices
as I drift at anchor into dream.

Hollow water clunks and bubbles, and awakens me,
but it is not morning. The wet air rests low and large,
boisterous with jabber
in the over-arching branches that net the sky
with tangled moonlight capturing sounds
of words from the opposite shore.

An aluminum skiff approaches
holding a man and woman who chatter and jostle
like two June bugs on a rusted wire screen.
The man stands, half turning to lift an ice chest,
but loses his balance and falls into frothy water,
a woman reaching out to grasp his hand.

Drifting closer, they rearrange themselves
engaged in friendly argument, directing one another
to do this or that above the flat and blank pale creek
moving under the raw moon's light.

When they notice me, they're startled. The man
sits at the outboard engine, the woman stoops forward
at the bow, the skiff erupting with a huff, leaning and churning
full bore upstream into the dark megaphone of the night.
They disappear in a meringue of sputters,
the buttery surface lapping along the fringe of shadow.

In the morning, I continue to row toward a maze of docks
sculpted and cabled in concrete with studded pipes and spigots
strung with wire woven through hook and rusted clamp,

to a muscular catwalk swaying on the jointed planks
with a practical buoyancy.

Cottonwood snags reach up through the fog,
worn smooth and silver where the sparrows perch.
If time would stop, I would stop here, too.

THE RIVER AS TEACHER

In the grog of late afternoon,
cradled in the shade by arcs of high mud,
I watch an ultra-light airplane with yellow pontoons
tilt and waver around the bend, coming upriver
in bright dragonfly colors, the propeller pop-popping
with its chesty drone, the goggled pilot one long
silky scarf of red and gold.

Halfway down Diamond Island
I drop the anchor, pay out line and tie up to a stump
under branches, to sleep in shoal waters speckled with snags.

Sunrise pools up over distant hills and treetops
spreading out as if from some deep wound, the great sun
rising from the ground, a circular coal shimmering in waves
of steamy reds. Like a bruised plum, it hovers
beyond the smokestack's silhouette, a curved knife splitting
its fiery doors, quivering with that first mist of earthly light.

Quickened colors bend my gaze
into the immediacy of boat and oars, of feet and legs,
the damaged light rising into a scenic warning
as if from some wild voice.

My hands hold pain in crescent finger bones
and scavenge like crabs melting into flesh around the oars
strengthening with the lengthening wake
—a seepy-eyed sunrise running fast in daggered light,
the source of all my red silence.

Today, the burnt tree
has shattered into a flock of brittle birds
breaking from a place I was not meant to be.

A fear warps from murky night, but lasts only so long.
Freed into an earthly motion, I row away on the water
that broadens with heat and widens into flame.

On a gunnel, the hot blue spark of a damselfly
changes my perspective to an oar, showing me
how to move, darning my spirit to the gentler tasks.

Then it darts off, skimming above the cupped surface
in its little puff of wind.

With tutorage, I cross the metallic lake
to a river town rimmed with fleeted barges, miles stretching
before and around, Pelican shrinking into the immense
bronze emptiness.

Beaver signs weave through willows, a channel buoy
hangs from a tree, and a five-foot gar suns itself, spooking
into splashes when I pass. Sandbars are birthing more islands,
wetlands sheltering ducks in the animated reeds.

The mosquitoes tumble out from the foliage,
swarming into a tapestry where the silver carp rise
like little moons over the anchorage.

I close the canvas and light the lantern,
splotching the inside of my cocoon maroon with blood.

100 Miles of Heat

The earth cares for us if we let it,
but riddles seem our usual response:

a river without water; food we cannot eat;
water we cannot drink; a swim we cannot take.

Visions sharpen into cutting.
The morning becomes unmercifully clear.

So I row and row.

Coal companies keep Uniontown working.
Towboats wait, idling downriver off Poker Point, stacked up
in line for the locks. One, a tow full of coal and as long
as an island, stretches upriver and takes five minutes to pass
in its deep trough of elephant feet.

I row through farmlands, over the shallow basin
of Wabash River gliding down with its load of silt
where pirates once lingered in the caves nearby
to prey upon the weak and unwary, the tired and naive.

In a single inhalation, the Ohio expands to a mile,
rippling past sandbars birthing islands from hidden channels
that flow darkly over fallen trees as regal as Shivas,
the deep pools bubbling with fish, and solar vats reflecting
the hem between earth and sky.

In this vast space heat lifts into a vacuum,
a distant diesel engine churning and bending out of sight.

Splintered into gray wood, Shawneetown is a terminal
for coal barges, blistered trailers, and a silent mutt guarding
an empty bar. All the people have gone somewhere else.

On the burnt grass of a deserted park, I find a pipe
with a spigot that works. Hot water at first, then warm,
then cool gallons pouring over my head, my back and neck,
puddling into the broad flat brown of grass and dirt.

The day ends with blue herons that circle, stalking
the twilight, or stand motionless on the limbs of snag,
tungsten feathers merging with shadow, eyes concentric
yellow rims, toes as thick as fingers.

Inside the canvas, the dark fills with hieroglyphics,
with abstract paintings in splotches and smears—an array
of reds in the quieting.

In the morning, Pelican whispers away.
By noon, the shoreline lengthens into limestone cliffs,
into huge blocks stacked as a levee built by giants
where I'm espied by eagles and pirates in ambush
behind the high crest of twisted cedars.

At Cave-in-the-Rock, I forage for cool drinks, and walk
up through a dusty woodland. It is a real snake day.
They rustle in the dried leaves—garter snakes all charged up,
vibrating their joys, flashing down to a coolness of burrow
in the knotted roots of maple and pine.

At the hillcrest, a line of dwarf red cedar shades a restaurant,
the river lazing below, glazed by the kiln of the sun.

When I return, the dory sits high and dry, poised on a mud bar
like a big white marshmallow.

Swirling the oar I spoon through cottonwood shade
past an old Fish Market, past the end of its sagging catwalk
with its floating shanty that tilts beneath the falling sun
curving gently down its swayed back, past the landing
stagnant now with cobwebs and beer cans,
to anchor well off Plew Island, heading upstream.

Each night hides a coming day. Strong river currents
narrow between rocky ledges and shoulder into curves, shearing
past inactive quarries and canyons of silent stone.

Ghosts of machines echo in a hewn valley, in a radiant
unfinished landscape from some ancient abandoned city
where hand tools, buckets, blue shirts, and lunch pails
still exist as a form of light—the translucent workers walking
home past barges rusting into scrap on the amiable shore,
smooth orange stones crazed by Kentucky heat.

I'd like to take a swim, and cool down,
but not in this shimmering sluice, this metallic mirage
as caustic as any chemical drum, where a serrated river cuts
at the bleeding of the world. Thin and malleable,
it spills uncertainties beneath the uninhabitable blue sky.

Hammered by the heat, I retreat into a motel room
at Golconda Marina, air-conditioned where the chrome shines,
scattered with little soaps and shampoos on a pink countertop
and enough towels to shower all day.

I visit the town, alongside a road crackling underfoot like ash.
I meld into the crowd to glimpse a face or gather a glance,
to recover myself on the street, storing up bits of dialogue
in this hiatus from which I must depart.

The sun falls onto the anvil. People have died in the cities.

ELYSIUM SHOALS

I anchor above the up-whelming earth
that keeps the coyotes howling and cattle bellowing,
the river level dropping to a mussel shell
at arm's length, the sand bursting into nicks
of oar bumping over the bottom.

But what is my hurry? I can just walk
through the morning on low bars of shell and rock
towing the dory, wading through these cool waters
of Elysium shoals, the Ohio stretching across forever
beneath the hawk toward my journey's end.

There is no worry in the being here for the doing.

Off Ledbetter Light three channels converge,
the shuttle towboats grooming loads of fleeted barges,
darting-in like bees to a bouquet of big black roses.
Petroleum piers stud the city side, the river clogged
with commercial activity as I edge past on tiptoe,
tires swarming above on the metal grid of a bridge,
the dory's white hull a speck on the tan wide river

—a water strider enlivened by every tiny effort.

A LEVEE TOWN

I clear the Grand Bar, the sun a burnished disk
above the gaudy gambling town of Metropolis.
A lone paddlefish, like an ICBM, launches
over the waste pits of Allied Chemical and Dye
squared off into sections for evaporation,
the floodplain furry with bayou and swamp.

The click and buzz of cicadas sink into a spell,
a roulette wheel spinning above the flat green waters.

A skiff with an excited fisherman
stops to show his winnings, his boat filled with catfish:
all four eighty-pounders each with huge shovel heads,
curving mouths, whiskers the size of pencils,
hides like pale clouds moved by the slick scythes
of their tails; his happiness an incredible surprise.

I wonder how many chips he'll need to eat those fish.
He speeds off promising garden tomatoes.

Joppa is a levee town nestled a half-mile back
from watermarks twenty feet up in the cottonwoods.
Lunch is served southern style at the Mid-Day Café,
in the living room of a home on Main Street.

When I return to the dory, there's a paper sack
full of fresh tomatoes. Just as you think you know,
the answer finds you out.

I sweep into the easy arms of a mile-wide river,
a pack of dogs jogging along on the gun metal beach
beneath the broad shoulders of a power station.

The map shows a navigable depth, so I line up
parallel to the old dam's guide wall, rowing for steerage.

Although not plunging, the whitewater starts
to consume me, waves becoming fiery coals, curled chips
of blue steel overflowing the weir, a hot pointed tongue
singing of the steeplechase below. Until, fleetingly,
there's a rasping, a hidden gargling as if all of this
might suddenly end in a swallowing.

I bound through the tines of sharpened sunset
piercing the evening hush beneath a bridge
that strides across the river on massive footings,
on concrete piers reinforced by ligaments of iron.

Yet there is no way I can become any smaller.
There is no way to slow the pacing of this world.

Last One Through

Old Dam 52
a submarine in the locks,
its rusty superstructure
and gold-pebbled walls,
the metal weir impassable,
barely overflowing.

I'm stepped down
awash in the friendly
hound dog pace
toward Fort Massac
where Lewis and Clark
recruited men, all able
and hearty, willing to imagine
a difference by the going.

Anchored above
in a creek dimpled by fish,
I fasten-up the canvas, thinking
that branches overhead
might allow a cottonmouth
to drop into the boat.

If only history were that pliable.

A Strong Cup of Tea

Towboats rattle in the gloom of my fatigue.
By evening, without a place to anchor, I'm worried,
but think I'm going to make it to the next creek,
an anchorage, where I'll feel safe for the night.
As I approach, I'm ambushed by scavenger flies
that bite and sting, like drops of acid. The boat veers.
I swat and slash with hands and towel my legs,
my neck and back. Infuriated,
I want to kill them all, and I'm getting good at it.
Carcasses pile up.

I'd rather leave and slink away
from these flies, from this cattle-smelling land,
but it's dark and I'm tired,
the river wide and the far shore uncertain.
So I row up the broken brown water
to a fallen cottonwood, drop the stern anchor
and tie the bow to a limb.

Inside my cocoon, I keep killing flies, in handfuls:
enough to brew the devil a strong cup of tea.
The creek reeks of E. coli, and I'm surrounded
by strange words on the map, the sounds of slough
and bayou. And then I realize, I'm floating
in the center of a cattle-crossing.

And I can't believe it.
No one would be here by choice,
but here I am without the energy, or will to move.
I cannot depart. I have no greater desire
than to eat and rest,
and to fan myself with just the right flip
of my straw hat.

I am the smile of Mona Lisa on Humphreys Creek.

The Confluence

At Consolidated Grain, Pelican noses up onto mud
amid rocks and dead carp, the fishermen casting
baited hooks into shadows of silo and barge.

A raised highway links the river to a small town,
sequestered pines scattered along like lightening rods.

If there's a finish line, it's the railroad bridge
stretched between fleeted barges and a stone quay,
a breakwater protecting the apartment buildings
that brood over the city wharf with vacant eyeballs
bulging with gray clouds from the red brick walls.

A halting serenity approaches an anxious intensity
in the largest joining of fresh water in the United States.

Nestled into a curve of riprap, I anchor.
Towboats sweep the shoreline with their searchlights
locating mile markers or numbered barges
to restructure their load. Moths bump in the darkness.

Awakened under the moon, I sit flayed by the beams
of a shuttle towboat cabling new loads near the State Park's
public ramp. Surprised to find me here, he warns me off
with a loud PA system from his wheelhouse.

He wants his commercial freedoms. I demand my public rights.
He rustles space in the middle of the night. I stay vigilant,
the canvas down, the anchor up, and both oars poised
until his foray ends, and the towboat careens back upriver
squealing in its white wake.

An Empty City

In a city full of bad weather
everyone has moved away, houses sell for payments
abandoned or foreclosed, mailboxes flapping open.

But the Greyhound Bus still stops at the gas station
on Tuesdays, so in a few days I'll catch a ride
to the closest city with a rental truck.

A hundred humid clouds are churning,
a wind-shear dragging everything from the south
up over the roofs of banks and past the face
of the old town's clock tower.

The horizon pops up into a squall
slipping along the ground like a steam iron or anvil
on slanted rain. Sharp wedges clash into echoes
beneath the bridge, vicious winds
snap branches, tilt people over, and hammer
summer grass as lightening whips
the painted animals escaping a carousel.

Gusts swirl at the confluence where two rivers meet.
Then, it all stops. People pull their boats onto trailers,
trailers up the ramp, and I lift the dory from a rock
re-anchoring farther out in the mud.

That night, I keep my rendezvous
with the towboat rustling barges under the moon.
We exchange blazes from our lanterns:
his more powerful; mine more attuned
to the flickers in the cave.

A Final Flower

Memory is a flower holding tightly to its stem,
the past a mile-wide river growing thin, continuing
to build sand into more and more islands.

Time and distance strengthen, connecting earth to sky.
Voices close to paradise in the wilderness of the mind.

A yearning for that balance, or perhaps a wishful dream.

The Ohio becoming a desert, a riddle human-made.
The Beautiful River the origin to a journey we need.

Over cut lengths of PVC, the dory rolls up the ramp
into the rental truck, like a capstone to a pyramid.

I drive through rainstorms,
between colorful facets of prismatic blindness
and a funnel of yellow lines brimming with headlights.

Turning off at the first exit
no longer able to see, I bend sideways like a willow
to sleep, breathing a final flower of the Oyo,

the fantasy frogs singing amid late night camp voices.

About the Author

photo: Sandie Seeger

Mark B. Hamilton is perhaps the only living person to have traced the entire Lewis and Clark Expedition route on their approximate time-table, traveling as they did by paddle and pack mule, from Pittsburgh, Pennsylvania, to the Pacific Ocean, and the return to St. Louis, Missouri—a 3-year, 8,000-mile journey. Honored in recognition by the National Park Service, his efforts in this field continue with research and writings centered on cultural environmental values.

He has been a shipwright, English professor, editor, and caseworker for Children and Youth Services. Born in Hartford, Connecticut, and raised in the small town of North Granby, he attended university at Miami, San Diego, and Missoula, earning the MFA in poetry with extensive work in literature and American studies from the Writers Workshop, University of Montana.

His poetry has won state and national awards, being published widely in the US, and abroad in the UK, Japan, Greece, Germany, and Austria. Select honors include: a Matthew Hansen Endowment for Wilderness Studies, the National Panhandler Chapbook Award, a National Poetry Anthology Contest Award, an Indiana State National Endowment for the Arts for Visiting Artists, an Indiana Governor's Award, and two Colorado Annual Poetry Awards, along with a readership at the American Antiquarian Society, and literary fellowships at UCROSS and the Center for Art & Ecology.

— markhamilton98643@yahoo.com
— www.MarkBHamilton.WordPress.com

SHANTI ARTS

NATURE ▪ ART ▪ SPIRIT

Please visit us online
to browse our entire book catalog,
including poetry collections and fiction,
books on travel, nature, healing, art,
photography, and more.

Also take a look at our highly
regarded art and literary journal,
Still Point Arts Quarterly, which
may be downloaded for free.

www.shantiarts.com